3/03
57

P9-EKX-065

WITHDRAWN

PAPIER MÂCHÉ

Barrie Caldecott

Consultant: Henry Pluckrose

Photography: Chris Fairclough

FRANKLIN WATTS
New York/London/Toronto/Sydney

Copyright © 1992 Franklin Watts

Franklin Watts, Inc.
95 Madison Avenue
New York, NY 10016

Library of Congress Cataloging-in-Publication Data

Caldecott, Barrie.
    Papier mâché / by Barrie Caldecott.
        p.   cm. — (Fresh start)
    Includes bibliographical references and index.
    Summary: Provides step-by-step instructions for making different
items out of paper mâché, including a vase, puppets,
and candlestick.
    ISBN 0-531-14217-5
    1. Papier mâché—Juvenile literature. [1. Paper mâché.
2. Handicraft.] I. Title. II. Series: Fresh start (London)
TT871.C35   1993   92-6259
745.54'2—dc20   CIP AC

Design: Edward Kinsey

Editor: Jenny Wood

Typeset by Lineage Ltd,
Watford, England

Printed in Belgium

All rights reserved

Contents

Equipment and materials

This book describes activities which use the following:

Adhesive (gummed) dots
Aluminum pin dot mesh (12in×19in)
Balloons
Bottles (glass and plastic)
Bowls
Bradawl
Brooch pin
Brushes (for paste and paint)
Buttons
Candles
Candy wrappers
Cardboard (thick, thin and corrugated)
Cardboard box
Cardboard tubes
Casserole dish
Cling wrap
Colored tape
Compass
Craft knife
Cutting board
Double-sided tape
Dowel
Dressmaking pins
Drinking straws
Egg cartons (cardboard)
Elastic (shirring)
Electric blender
Feathers
Felt

Felt-tip pens
Garden wire
Gift wrapping ribbon
Glue (UHU)
Hole punch
Jello mold
Masking tape
Measuring cup
Modeling clay
Needle
Newspapers
Paint (gouache, household emulsion, poster and powder)
Paper (assorted colors, and one sheet of white, 12in×19in)
Paper tissues
Pastry cutter
Pencil
Petroleum jelly
Plastic sheet (or trash can liner)
Plates (old)
Pliers
Popsicle sticks
Rolling pin
Ruler
Sandpaper (fine)
Scissors
Sieve
String
Tablespoon
Teaspoon
Thread
Wallpaper paste
Water

One of the good things about papier mâché is that it is not expensive. Most of the materials you need count as household waste and so can be found at home. Rescue them before they are thrown away, and recycle them! Make a collection of newspapers, comics, cardboard boxes, egg cartons, toilet paper tubes and any used colored paper.

Before you start, cover your work space with newspaper and an opened-out trash can liner to protect the work surface.

Shaping your model

Most papier mâché models need an object on and around which to build the model's basic shape. This object can be some form of removable mold, or a structure that is left inside the finished model. The projects in this book use molds and structures such as plastic and glass bottles, plates, wire mesh, balloons, casserole dishes, cardboard and modeling clay. All these objects are easily available, at no great cost.

Removing a mold

Where a mold is to be removed, some kind of releasing method is needed. There are three main methods. The first is to wipe the inside of the mold with petroleum jelly before adding the papier mâché mixture. The second is to cover the mold with cling wrap. The third and final method involves laying the first layer of papier mâché right onto the mold. No glue is used, but the newspaper needs to be made wet enough so that the first layer stays in place while the rest of the pasted layers are added.

Glue

There are three main types of glue for making papier mâché: wallpaper paste, PVA, and cold water paste powder (starch paste). The most easily available and the most economical is wallpaper paste. To make a suitable mix, follow the instructions on the box or package.

Most wallpaper pastes contain a fungicide which may cause irritation to sensitive skin and should not be used by young children. A pair of rubber gloves (obtainable from the drugstore or market) can be worn to avoid this problem. It is possible to buy starch powder paste without fungicide from educational suppliers, craft stores and some hardware stores.

When using PVA, mix equal quantities of glue and water.

Preparing the paper
When making papier mâché, always tear rather than cut the newspaper. The rough edges will feather and smooth down when pasted, whereas cut edges show up as lines. Use small pieces of paper for sharp corners and curves, and large pieces for large, rounded areas. Have a bowl of water handy to wet the paper before it is pasted into position on complex models. (Wetting the paper is important as this softens the paper and makes it easier to bend and mold around corners and curves.) When more than one layer of papier mâché is required, use two colors of newspaper (white and pink, or white and colored newsprint from a comic), as this method will help you keep track of the layers.

Drying your model
When covered with the required number of papier mâché layers, the model should be left to dry evenly, near a radiator if possible. No times are given for drying, as these can vary considerably depending on temperature, number of layers and humidity.

Painting your model
The paint for the first coat of color on the papier mâché should be matte household emulsion. This will cover up the newsprint, strengthen the papier mâché and leave a good surface for decoration. You can make your own colored emulsion by mixing powder paint or gouache into small quantities of white emulsion.

None of the projects in this book use oil- or spirit-based paints as these take longer to dry, but if you want a more hard-wearing finish, papier mâché can be painted with enamels and clear varnish to give a glossy look.

Here, a plate is used to provide the basic shape.

You will need newspapers (two different colors), two plates (one for the model, and one on which to "paste up" the newspaper pieces), a pencil, scissors, water, brushes for paste and paint, paste, white emulsion paint, powder paint or gouache, a compass, a ruler, a cutting board, a craft knife, thick cardboard, garden wire, pliers, masking tape, cling wrap, colored tape, adhesive dots, and a picture.

1 Tear out ten sheets of newspaper (five of each color). Lay the "modeling" plate on each sheet in turn and draw around it, about ½in out from the plate's edge. Cut out the ten circles.

2 Lay one newspaper circle on the "pasting up" plate. Wet the circle thoroughly, then gently press it down onto the "modeling" plate. Press flat any small creases. Fold each of the remaining nine circles three times, so that each circle is divided into eight triangular sections. Tear along the crease lines, then paste the 72 pieces onto the "modeling" plate, on top of the first circle. Use the "pasting up" plate to brush the pieces with your paste mixture before adding them to the model. (Once each newspaper piece is in position on the model, smooth it down with the paste brush.) Overlap the pieces by about ¾in, and have them just touching at the center. Leave to dry.

3 Trim off the rough edge. Then remove the papier mâché plate and paint it with a coat of white emulsion.

4 Using the compass, find the center of the papier mâché plate and draw four circles in roughly the positions shown. Draw a square around the central circle. The size of the central circle should be such that, when you draw the square around it, the edges of the square remain within the flat part of the plate. Draw a pattern (similar to that shown) between the second and third circles.

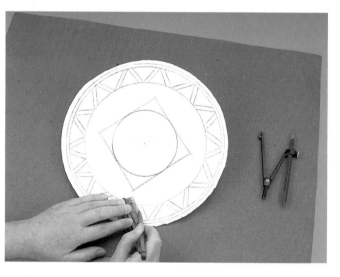

5 Use the craft knife to cut out the square and the sections of pattern, as shown. Always cut *away from* the hand that is holding the plate down. Trim around the line of the outer circle, to form the outside edge.

6 Paint the papier mâché plate in a bright color.

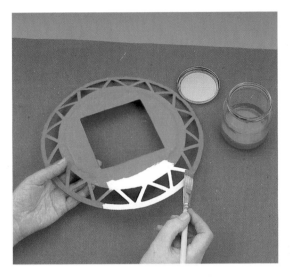

7 Lay the painted plate on top of a piece of thick cardboard, and draw around the edges of the square. Remove the plate, then draw two more squares. The edges of the second square should be ½in outside the original, while the edges of the third square should be ¾in away. Cut around the third square, to form the outside edges of your cardboard piece. Then, using the edges of the second square as a guide, cut out the inside section of the cardboard piece. Paint the cardboard a different color than the plate.

8 Using the pliers, bend a piece of garden wire to form a hook, and tape it to an edge of the cardboard. Stretch cling wrap across the hole and attach it with masking tape.

9 Glue the cardboard to the back of the papier mâché plate, completing the picture frame. Decorate the front outer edge with the colored tape, and add some adhesive dots. Tape your chosen picture behind the cling wrap.

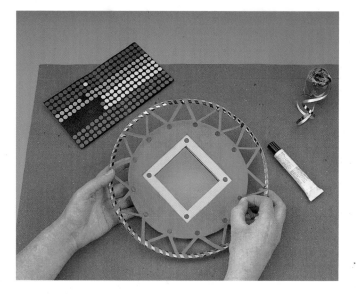

10 Experiment with different shapes of plate and different types of decoration.

Here an ordinary, large cardboard box is recycled into a smaller, more decorative one which can be used for storing precious objects.

You will need a sturdy cardboard box, a ruler, a pencil, scissors, a craft knife, a cutting board, glue (UHU), newspapers, paste, brushes for paste and paint, a "pasting up" plate, white emulsion paint, felt-tip pens, candy wrappers, and felt.

1 Cut up the cardboard box into the pieces shown. The pieces in the top row make up the lid (the semicircles form the handle), while the remainder are for the box and base. The base is 6in×4in (16cm×11cm) and the sides of the box are 5in×2½in (12cm×6cm) and 2½in×2½in (6cm×6cm). The 5½in×3½in (14cm×9cm) piece sits on top of the base, and forms the bottom of the box. The small pieces in the bottom row make the feet on which the base stands.

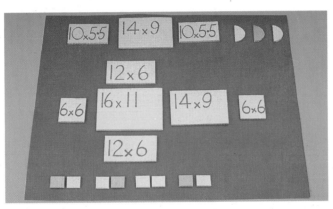

2 Glue the parts together as shown to form the box and lid. When making up the lid, note that one of the 4in×2in (10cm×5.5cm) cardboard pieces goes on top of the 5½in×3½in (14cm×9cm) piece, while the other is attached to the underside.

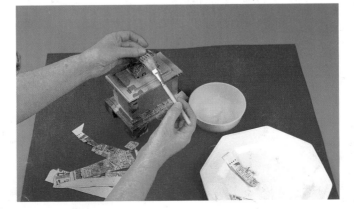

3 Cover all the exposed edges and joints with a layer of pasted-on torn newspaper strips. Make sure that the edges of the strips join together. Leave to dry.

4 Paint your box with two coats of white emulsion and decorate with felt-tip pens. Colored candy wrappers can be glued on for extra effect.

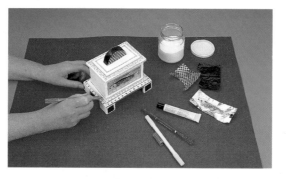

5 Cut some felt to line the inside of the box and lid, and glue in place.

6 You can use many different finishes and designs (the left-hand box is covered with aluminum foil, for example). You can change the appearance of the box, too. The barrel-shaped lid on the right-hand box is made from a sheet of thin cardboard, gently folded into position, then decorated with tissue paper.

A flower vase

It is difficult, for obvious reasons, to hold water in a papier mâché container. A colored plastic bottle is therefore used to line the inside of this vase.

You will need a 1.5 liter plastic bottle, scissors, a craft knife, a cutting board, masking tape, sheets of colored paper (several pink sheets and one green), paste, brushes for paste and paint, a "pasting up" plate, a plastic sheet or trash can liner, something to use as a weight, colored emulsion paint, and red gouache.

1 Remove the label, then wash and dry the bottle. Carefully cut off the top rounded part of the bottle using sharp scissors or the craft knife.

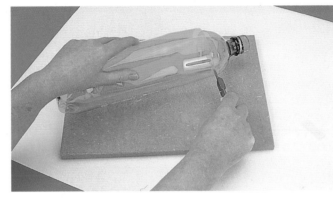

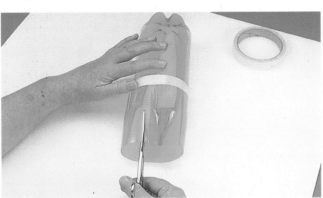

2 Wrap a strip of masking tape around the bottle, about two-thirds of the way up from the base. Using the scissors, cut strips ¼in wide from the top edge of the bottle down to the top edge of the masking tape.

3 Bend the strips back over the masking tape until they all stick out sideways.

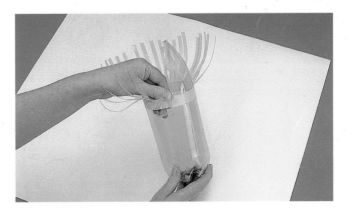

4 Remove the masking tape and paste a sheet of pink paper around the bottle. Cut the paper so that the bottom edge is straight, and lines up with the base of the bottle – otherwise, your vase will not be able to stand upright!

5 Place the bottle upside down on the plastic sheet, with the strips radiating outward. Put a weight on top of the base to keep it steady. Cut or tear some triangular strips of pink paper. Each strip should be approximately 8in high and 4in across the base. Bend up the pointed end of each strip to a length of about 2½in from the point. Attach the strips to the bottle, as shown. Overlap them by about ½in on the bottle and by about 1in on the outside edge. Leave to dry.

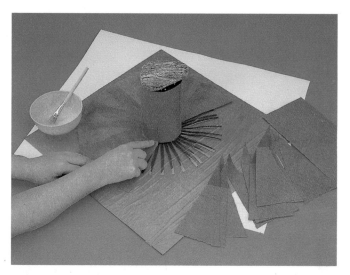

6 Paint the tips of the plastic strips with colored emulsion. Paint lines of red gouache on the pink triangular strips and cut out petals around them as shown.

7 Cut three long triangles from the green paper, each about 12in×4in. Fold each triangle in half, and make a firm crease line down the center. Open the triangles out and glue them around the base, as shown.

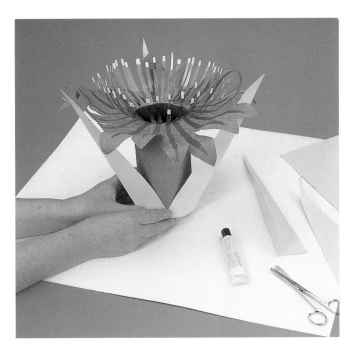

8 Many different kinds of vases and flowers can be made. Look at some books on flowers to give you ideas, and work with bottles of different shapes and sizes.

A colorful bangle

This project uses stiff cardboard to make a simple decorative bangle.

You will need a metal ruler, a pencil, thick cardboard (approximately 8in×14in), scissors, a compass, a craft knife, glue (UHU), newspapers, paste, brushes for paste and paint, a "pasting up" plate, colored emulsion paint, and gouache or poster paints (various colors).

1 Clench your hand as if you were going to put on a bracelet. Now place your clenched hand on a flat surface, as shown, and measure the height from the surface to the top edge of your hand. Draw a square on the piece of cardboard, with sides twice this measurement. Cut out the square.

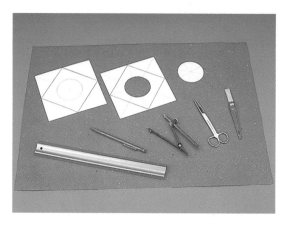

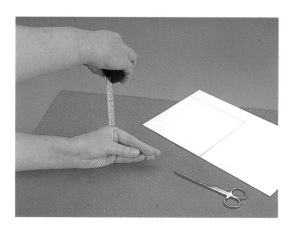

2 Divide up the square as shown. Using the compass, draw a circle in the center of the square. The diameter of the circle should be the same measurement as the height of your clenched hand. Score along the edges of the inner square, and cut out the circle. Now make a second, identical cardboard piece.

3 Lay the two cardboard pieces on top of each other, as shown. Bend the triangles along the scored lines at an angle of about 45° and in the directions shown, then glue the two pieces together.

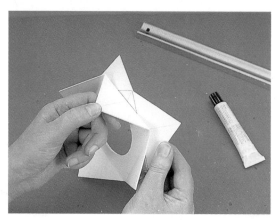

4 Cut four ½in cardboard squares. Cut each square in half diagonally, then glue the eight triangle shapes onto the model in the positions shown.

5 Paste strips of newspaper ¾in wide across the gaps, as shown. Use two layers. Leave to dry.

6 Paint your bangle, using colored emulsion.

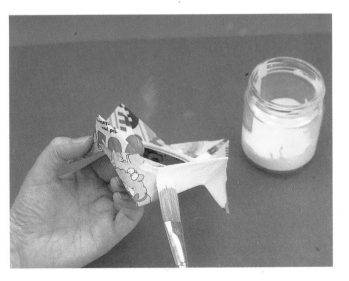

7 Decorate your bangle, using a variety of patterns and designs.

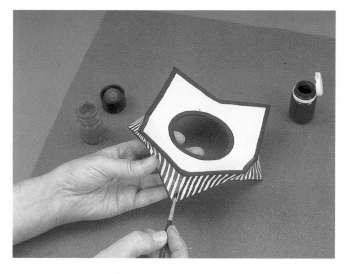

8 Experiment with different bangle shapes.

A piggy bank

The basis of this model is a balloon.

You will need a round balloon, string, a cardboard tube about 3½in long, masking tape, scissors, newspapers, paste, brushes for paste and paint, a "pasting up" plate, four cardboard tubes (each about 1½in in diameter×2½in long), thick cardboard, a dressmaking pin, white emulsion paint, a craft knife, a pencil, gouache or poster paints, and a felt-tip pen.

1 Blow up the balloon and knot the end. Tie a piece of string around the knot. Pull the string through the long cardboard tube and hold it in position by taping the end to the outside of the tube, as shown.

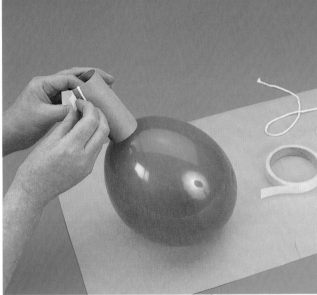

2 Attach the tube to the balloon by pasting small strips of newspaper around the join. Then cover the whole balloon with six layers of papier mâché. Leave to dry.

3 To form the legs of your piggy bank, tape the four short cardboard tubes onto the balloon in the positions shown. Tape on a length of cardboard (about ¼in×8in) for the tail. Cut and attach cardboard triangles for ears.

4 To form the pig's nose, cut the long cardboard tube so that it is between ¾in and 1in long (but don't cut through the string). Using the pin, pop the balloon inside the papier mâché. Draw out the bits of balloon by pulling the string. Join all the pig's legs and ears permanently to its body with two layers of newspaper strips. Cover over the ends of the nose and legs, too. Leave to dry.

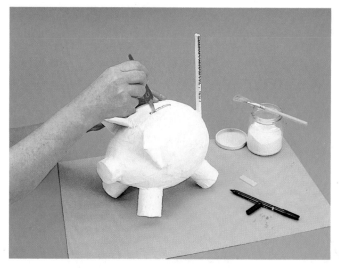

5 Paint with a coat of white emulsion. When dry, mark a coin slot in the top of the pig and carefully cut this out with the craft knife.

6 Roll the tail around the pencil to make it curly. Now paint the whole pig's body with pink gouache. When dry, use a felt-tip pen to add the pig's features. Paint on flowers or other decorations.

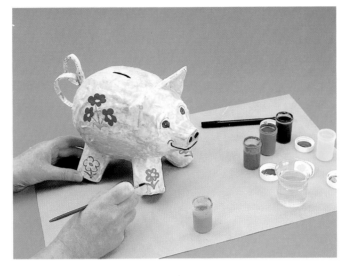

7 Many different balloon shapes are available. The wobbly clown was made with a pear-shaped balloon and a cone of paper. It is weighted inside at the bottom with a stone. The space monster was made with a frankfurter-shaped balloon and cardboard tubes.

This is a pulp technique that uses a bear-shaped mold, but you can use any shape of mold you have available.

You will need an electric blender, water, a measuring cup, a sheet of newspaper, powder paint, a tablespoon, a sieve, two bowls, a Jello mold, petroleum jelly, PVA glue, paper tissues, fine sandpaper, gouache or poster paints (various colors), and a paintbrush.

1 ASK AN ADULT TO HELP YOU WITH THIS. Pour one pint of water into the blender. Add a 24in × 16in sheet of newspaper which has been torn into small pieces, and add a tablespoonful of powder paint. Blend until the mixture looks smooth and even.

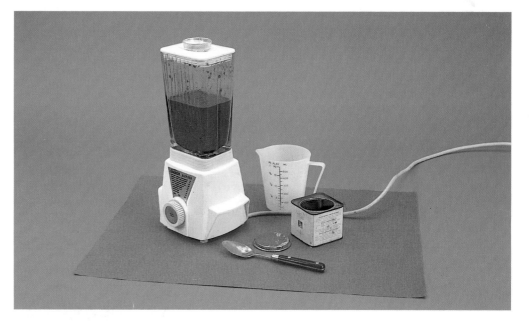

2 Rest the sieve over one of the bowls. Pour the contents of the blender into the sieve and leave for about five minutes, to allow the excess water to drain out.

3 Rub a layer of petroleum jelly around the inside of the mold. Tip the contents of the sieve into the second bowl, and mix two tablespoonsful of PVA glue into the pulp. Fill two-thirds of the mold with this mixture. Tap the mold gently to level the pulp and eliminate any air bubbles. If your mold needs more pulp than you have made, repeat steps 1, 2 and 3 until you have the required amount.

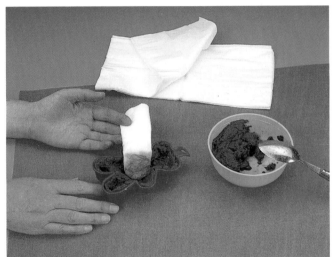

4 Using your fingers, press the pulp up the sides and down into the curves of the mold until the pulp is about ¼in thick all over. Place a piece of paper tissue into the lowest part of the mold and hold it there for a few minutes to absorb any excess water. Leave the mold near a radiator to allow the pulp to dry.

5 Remove the dried pulp from the mold and use the sandpaper to smooth down any rough edges.

6 Decorate your molded shape in an appropriate way, to suit the type of mold you have used.

7 Use molded shapes as the basis for other objects. Here the bear has been used as the basis of a toy clock.

Glass bottles make excellent candleholders. This one is decorated using a wax resist technique.

You will need any glass bottle with a neck suitable for holding a candle, thick cardboard, a pencil, scissors, a craft knife, a cutting board, masking tape, newspapers, paste, brushes for paste and paint, a "pasting up" plate, corrugated cardboard, glue (UHU), colored emulsion paint, a candle, and gouache.

1 Wash and dry the bottle. Cut a circle (trace around the base of the bottle) from the cardboard. Using the craft knife, cut four slits across the center of the circle, each about 1in long.

2 Push the center of the cardboard circle over the mouth of the bottle until the circle is resting about ¾in down from the top. Hold in position with masking tape.

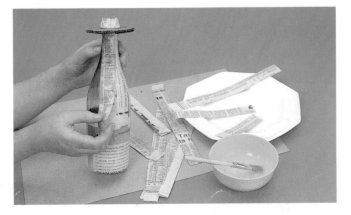

3 Paste about ten long, thin strips of newspaper around the mouth of the bottle to cover the join with the cardboard circle. Cover the main part of the bottle with two layers of newspaper strips. Leave to dry.

4 Cut a strip of corrugated cardboard about 2½in wide×12in long and wrap it around the cardboard circle, corrugated side out. Mark the place where the ends of the strip overlap. Cut off any excess and glue the strip to the cardboard circle so that the top of the strip is level with the top of the bottle. Hold the ends of the strip in place with masking tape while the glue dries.

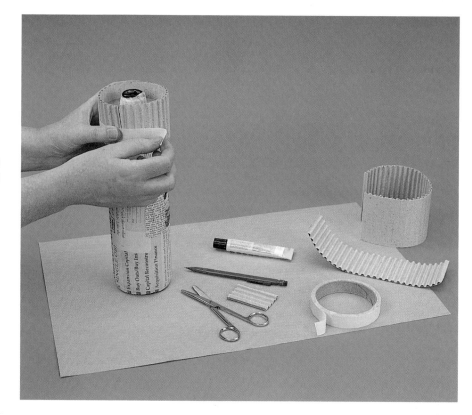

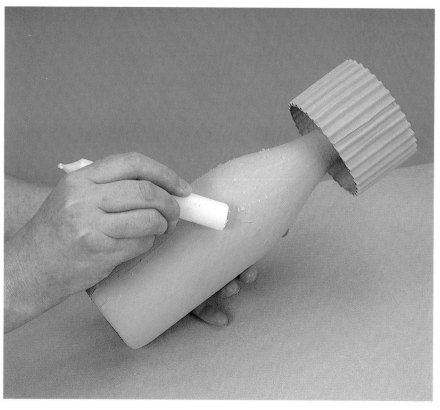

5 Paint the whole model with a light-colored emulsion. When dry, draw the edge of the base of the candle down the side of the bottle, leaving trails of wax.

6 Paint the bottle and the cardboard circle again, in a darker color. This time, use gouache. Leave the corrugated cardboard strip in its original color, but add lines of the darker color for effect.

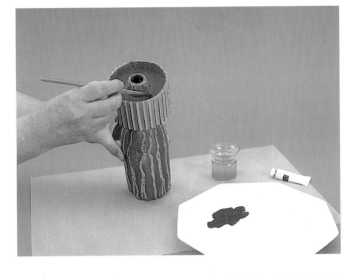

7 Experiment with other constructions. The Father Christmas is made from crumpled paper taped in place and covered with more strips of paper.

A casserole dish can be used as a mold to make a variety of masks. Here is one example.

You will need an oval casserole dish with an opening of about 5½in×8in, a sheet of plastic, cling wrap, a cardboard egg carton, scissors, glue (UHU), newspapers, paste, brushes for paste and paint, a "pasting up" plate, colored emulsion paint, a pencil, a ruler, three sheets of colored paper (each one a different color), shirring elastic, gift ribbon, masking tape, and gouache or poster paints.

1 Lay the dish, open side down, on the sheet of plastic. Cover the surface of the dish with cling wrap. Cut up the egg carton to make the ears, nose, eyebrows and mouth, as shown. Position the ears midway up the sides of the dish and align the ends of the eyebrows with the tops of the ears.

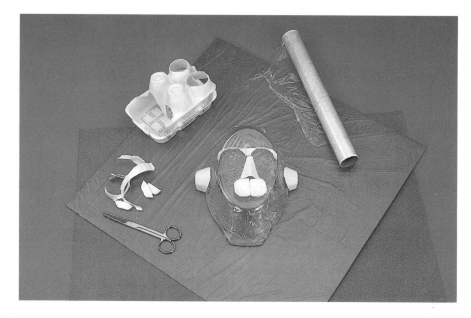

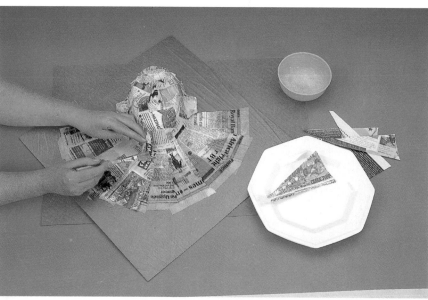

2 Cover the dish with five layers of papier mâché. Paste strips of newspaper (about 6in long) over the sheet of plastic, too, as shown, working around the top half of the dish, above the ears. Leave to dry.

3 Remove the dish and paint the mask with a coat of emulsion. Mark about ten spikes around the headdress part of the mask, and cut out as shown. Cut out two holes for the eyes.

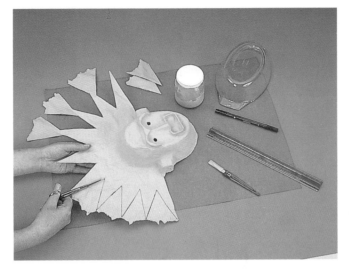

4 Lay the mask on a sheet of colored paper. Trace around the headdress outline, adding about ½in to the height and width of the spikes as you do so. Cut out the spiked shape. Do this with the remaining two sheets of colored paper, giving each one larger spikes than before.

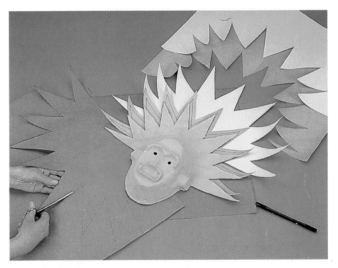

5 Glue the three colored shapes together, as shown.

6 Glue the extra spikes to the mask. Cut away the overlap on the inside of the mask. Attach a piece of elastic through a hole in each ear. Glue a bundle of gift ribbon (held together with masking tape) to the end of each spike.

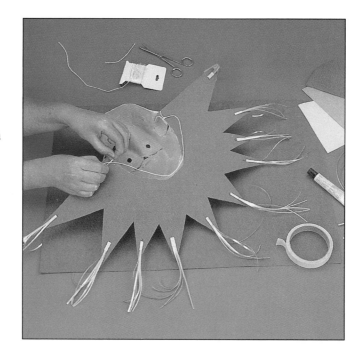

7 Decorate the mask in any way you like. Think of the different effects masks can create.

For this simple but effective piece of jewelry you will need an electric blender, water, a measuring cup, newspapers, powder paint, a tablespoon, a sieve, two bowls, PVA glue, a rolling pin, a cutting board, modeling clay, a shaped cookie cutter, a button, a drinking straw, a pencil, a teaspoon, a paper tissue, fine sandpaper, colored emulsion paint, paintbrushes, double-sided tape, candy wrappers, a hole punch, gouache or poster paints, a brooch pin, and thin cardboard or oak tag.

1 Make a quantity of pulp, following the method described on pages 22 and 23. Roll out some modeling clay to form a piece about ¼in thick and slightly larger than the cookie cutter. Place the clay on a sheet of newspaper and gently press the cookie cutter into it. (Do not press right through to the paper.)

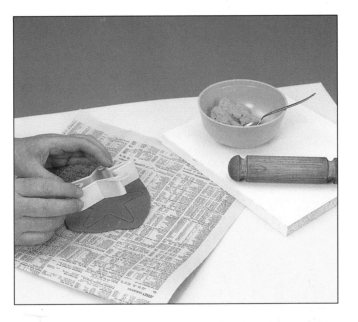

2 Place the button in the center of the shape, like a "jewel." Using the straw, press right through to the paper to form holes around the "jewel." Make more holes around the edge of the shape.

3 Remove the "jewel." Reposition the cookie cutter on the clay and this time press right through to the paper. Remove the cookie cutter, making sure that the clay shape is attached. Put some pulp about ½in thick into the cookie cutter mold and press it down with the flat end of the pencil. Check that the pulp has gone down the holes in the clay by lifting the cookie cutter away from the newspaper.

4 Level the pulp, using the handle of the teaspoon. Place the paper tissue on top of the pulp for a few minutes to absorb any excess water. Keep the cookie cutter on the newspaper and leave in a warm place to allow the pulp to dry.

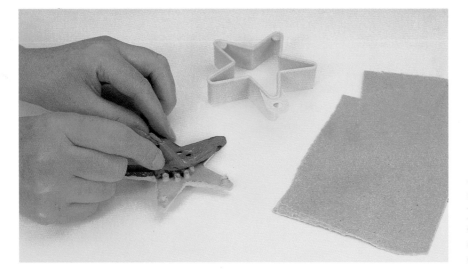

5 Push the dried pulp and clay out of the cookie cutter and peel off the clay. Smooth down any sharp edges with the sandpaper. Paint with a coat of emulsion.

6 Stick lengths of double-sided tape to the backs of different colored candy wrappers. Use the hole punch to make lots of small sticky dots.

7 Decorate your brooch with various colors of gouache or poster paint and add the sticky dots. Glue the "jewel" in position in the center.

8 Affix the brooch pin to the back of the brooch and glue a piece of thin cardboard over the open catch, as shown.

9 Many different cookie cutter shapes are available, so you can have fun making a whole range of brooches! You can even make earrings, too, by attaching an earring clip to a paper clip glued to the back of the decorated shape. The letters on the heart-shaped brooch were made by pressing the shapes M and E (in reverse) into the clay with a popsicle stick. (You need to reverse any letters so that they read correctly when the shape is removed from the mold.)

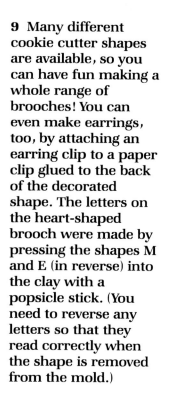

Using wire mesh it is possible to make a framework that can support lively and realistic papier mâché models. In this project, the structure of the dragon has been designed so that all the mesh is used.

You will need a large sheet of paper (12in×19in), a pencil, a ruler, aluminum pin dot mesh (12in×19in), scissors, masking tape, corrugated cardboard, paste, brushes for paste and paint, a "pasting up" plate, newspapers, thick cardboard, glue (UHU), a cardboard egg carton, green emulsion paint, gouache or poster paints (red and other colors), scrap paper, and red gift wrapping tape.

1 Copy this diagram onto the large sheet of paper. The diagram is constructed by dividing each side into four equal parts, the dotted line being the center line. The dotted line, therefore, should be positioned at the 6in point on the short edge of the paper. The other lines on this short edge should be drawn at 3in and 9in respectively. Along the long edge, the lines begin at 4¾in, 9½in and 14in. Where an unfinished line is shown, the point at which it stops is half-way to the next line. Copy the lines *exactly* as shown.

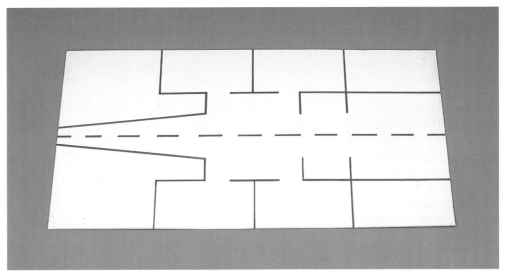

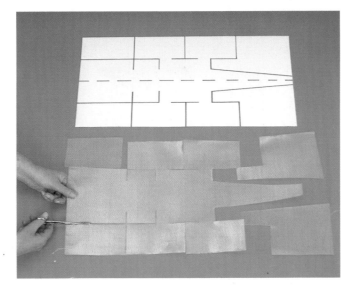

2 Place the wire mesh over the diagram and copy the lines onto it. Cut along all the lines as marked, *except for* the dotted line. The pieces of mesh that are cut off during this process will be used later.

3 Roll up the legs and head, and tape them into tubes using masking tape.

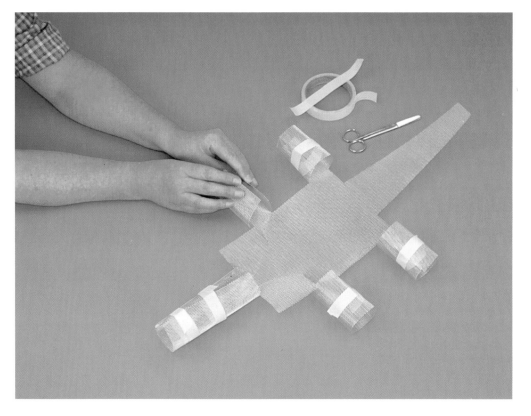

4 Bend the mesh so that the creature stands upright. Tape one of the small spare mesh rectangles into position to form the dragon's stomach, and cut two-thirds off the other to form the creature's chest. Roll two small tubes of corrugated cardboard and insert these into the dragon's nose to form nostrils. Cover the model with two layers of papier mâché. Leave to dry.

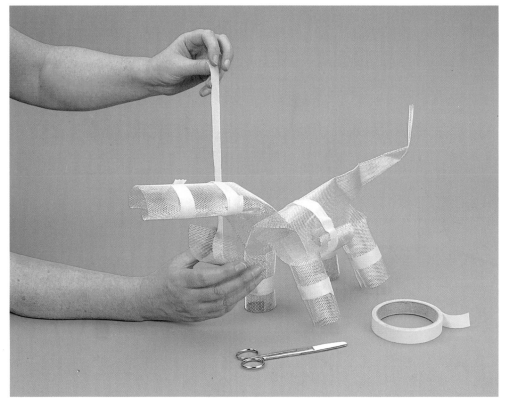

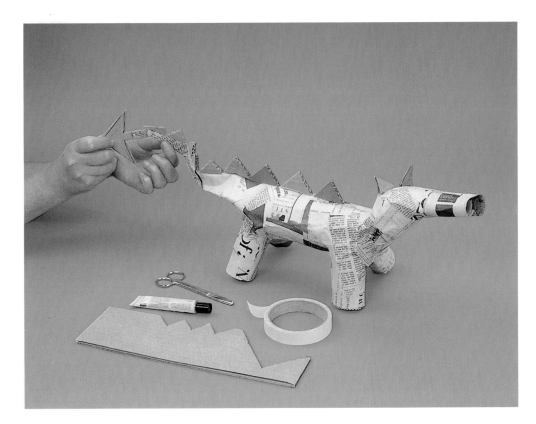

5 Cut an arrowhead and some triangles from the thick cardboard and glue these in position on the tail and along the spine. Glue on two more cardboard triangles for the ears.

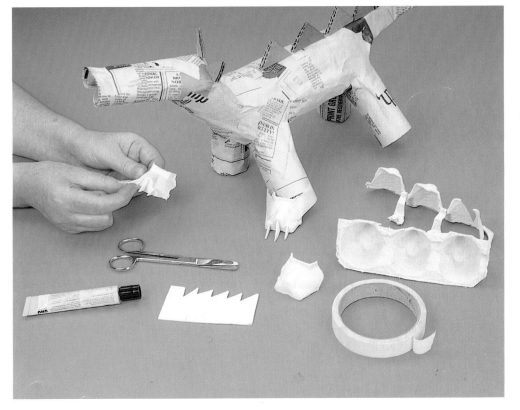

6 Cut out the sections from the egg carton to use as the dragon's feet. Hold these in position on the legs with masking tape. Glue triangular cardboard claws onto the feet.

7 Bend the flap of one of the wire mesh wing pieces at an angle and attach with masking tape to one shoulder. Attach the other wing piece to the other shoulder in the same way.

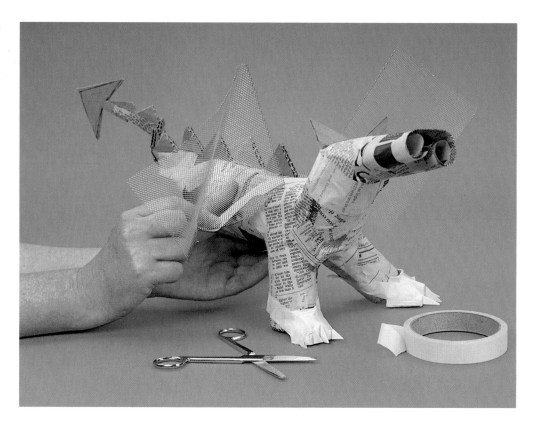

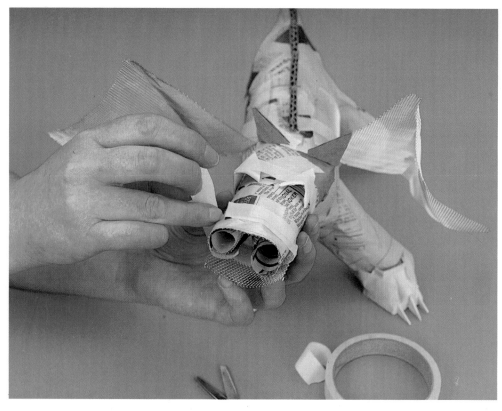

8 Tape the small remaining piece of wire mesh under the nostrils to form the dragon's lower jaw. Make eyes from the corners of the egg carton and tape these into position.

9 Cover all these additional parts of the model with two more layers of papier mâché. Allow it to dry, then paint the whole model with a coat of green emulsion. Add red scales.

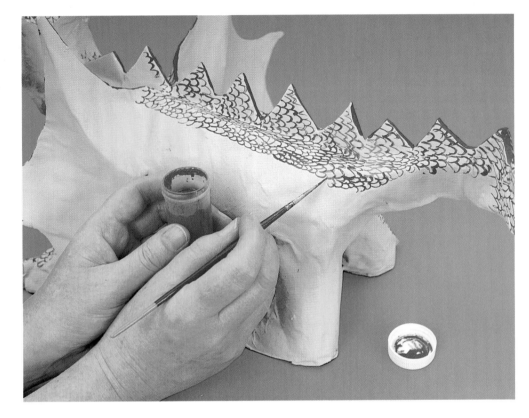

10 To finish, make and paint two rolls of scrap paper for the pupils and glue into the eyeholes. Cut two cardboard fangs and glue into position. Make some "flames" from lengths of the red gift wrapping tape and glue these into the dragon's mouth.

11 The finished model. You can try using the method described here to make larger objects. Work with chicken wire held together with garden wire, or use wood inside the wire mesh as a support for really big constructions.

A bird of paradise marionette

This model uses clay as the basis for the shape. The clay is later removed when the papier mâché has dried.

You will need modeling clay, a dowel rod, paste, brushes for paste and paint, a "pasting up" plate, newspapers, a craft knife, glue (UHU), scissors, masking tape, cardboard, a pencil, a ruler, drinking straws, garden wire, pliers, a bradawl, blue emulsion paint, gouache or poster paints (various colors), two popsicle sticks, a dressmaking pin, thread, a long needle, feathers, and buttons.

1 Make the head and body of the bird from modeling clay.

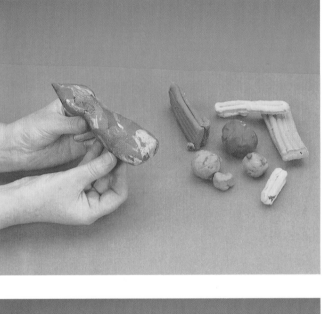

2 Press the dowel into the body and, using this as a handle, cover the head and body of the bird with five layers of papier mâché. Use torn pieces of newspaper about ¾in square.

3 Paste an additional six papier mâché layers (this time using pieces of newspaper about 2½in square) across the back of the body where the wings will go. The pieces should stick out at either side. Do the same for the tail, using triangular pieces about 2½in wide×3in high. Leave to dry.

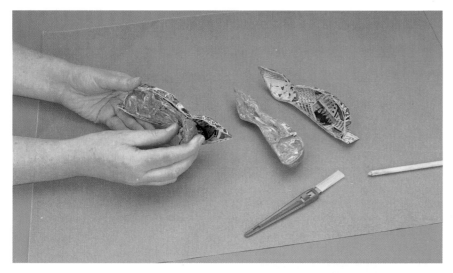

4 Remove the dowel and, using the craft knife, cut through the papier mâché into the clay. Cut down the middle of the body, making two equal halves. Carefully lift off the papier mâché shell from the clay.

5 Glue the two halves together with UHU and hold in place with masking tape. When dry, remove the tape and cover the join with a layer of newspaper strips. Leave to dry.

6 Cut two wings from the cardboard. Each wing should be about the same length as the body and head together. Cut a cardboard tail, too, equivalent to about one-third of the body and head length. Attach these to the body with masking tape, as shown. The masking tape is quite flexible and will act as a hinge.

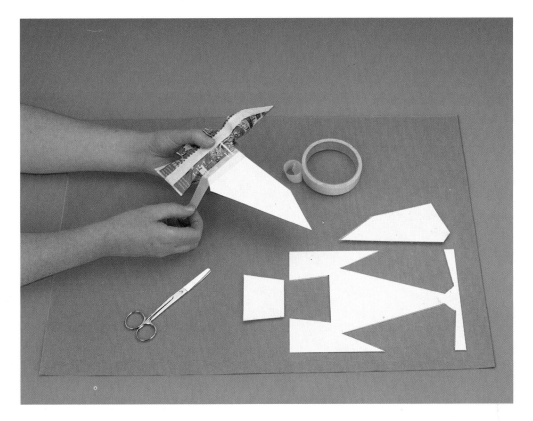

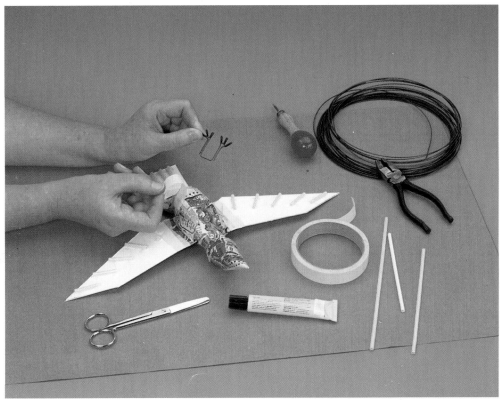

7 Cut fifteen 1in lengths of drinking straw. Glue five to each wing and five to the tail. Run glue over the straws to secure them. Using the pliers, bend a piece of garden wire to make the legs, and tape these to the underside of the body. Using the bradawl, pierce two holes toward the back of the head.

8 Paint the whole bird with blue emulsion and leave to dry. Use gouache or poster paint to decorate the wings in bright colors.

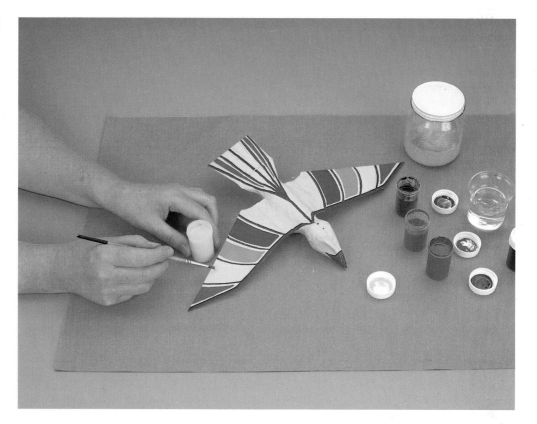

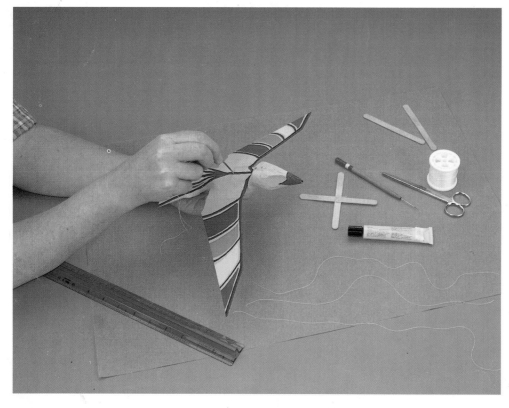

9 Glue and bind the two popsicle sticks together in the shape of a cross. Using the pin, pierce a hole in the middle of each of the wings. Pierce one hole in the tail and another through the center of the body. Cut four 16in lengths of thread and thread one length through each of the four holes (take about ¾in of thread through). Glue in position. (Use the long needle to pull the thread through the body).

10 Wrap the other ends of the threads around the sticks. The strings for the wings are wrapped around each end of one stick. The strings for the body and tail are wrapped around the other stick. Adjust the strings until the body and wings of the bird hang level. Glue in place.

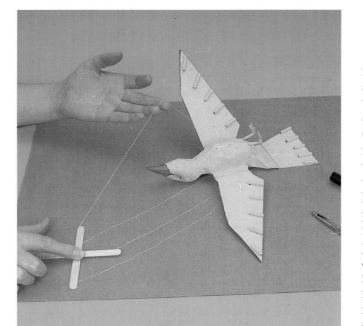

11 Insert and glue the feathers into the straws and into the two holes in the back of the bird's head. Glue on two buttons for eyes. It is possible to vary the shapes of the wings, tail, and head to make a pterodactyl or other flying creature. The process of using clay as the foundation for more complex marionettes is illustrated by the circus weightlifter.

Papier mâché objects have been made and used for centuries. Some are made from pulp, others from layers of paper, but all are classed as papier mâché.

The origin of the term "papier mâché" is unclear, as it seems to have been first used in seventeenth-century England rather than in France, as one might think. The Elizabethan word "mash," meaning "to mix with water," probably provides the term "mâché." But in French, the word "mâcher" means, literally, "to chew," and historians have found evidence of French workers coming to England to be employed specifically to chew paper in the papier mâché shops of London!

Whatever the origins of the name, the craft itself originated in China in the second century A.D. Papermaking was for centuries a long and expensive process (it was not until 1798 that Nicholas-Louis Robert invented machines to make paper). At first, rags and water were put into stone mortars and pounded with mallets until pulped. The Chinese used silk rags and old fishing nets as well as fiber from bamboo and mulberry trees. The pounding was done by hand. Because of this lengthy process, paper was reused whenever possible – hence the invention of papier mâché.

Papier mâché reached its heyday in the second half of the nineteenth century in Europe and America. It was used to make all kinds of objects, from snuff boxes and trays to furniture and panels of cabins on ocean liners. The strength and durability of papier mâché are shown by the survival to the present day of a Chinese warrior helmet hardened with lacquer, made in the second century A.D.

The use of papier mâché has declined since Victorian times, although the folk art tradition is still strong – particularly in China, India, Japan, and Mexico. Papier mâché is used, too, in carnivals, festivals and theaters because of its cheapness and lightweight qualities. Papier mâché is now reemerging as a craft used not only by school children but also by professional artists who have recognized its creative potential.

Most craft items used in this book can be obtained from stationery and/or art materials stores. Aluminum pin dot mesh for the dragon can be bought from home centers. The colored feathers for the mask and jewelry items can be bought from craft stores.

Helpful books

Bottomley, Jim. *Paper Projects for Creative Kids of All Ages.* Little, Brown & Co., 1983.

Corwin, Judith H. *Papercrafts.* Franklin Watts, 1988.

Capon, Robin. *Papier Mâché.* David Mass, 1977.

Crater, Michael. *Make it in Paper: Creative Three-Dimensional Paper Projects.* Dover, 1983.

Robson, Denny. *Masks and Funny Faces.* Gloucester, 1992.

PRINTED IN BELGIUM BY

INTERNATIONAL BOOK PRODUCTION